AF228148

FASCINATING FOOD

THE
FAST FOOD
INDUSTRY

BY LIZ SONNEBORN

Essential Library

An Imprint of Abdo Publishing
abdobooks.com

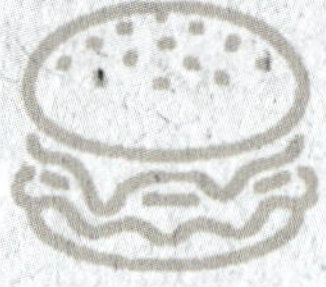

ABDOBOOKS.COM

Published by Abdo Publishing, a division of ABDO, PO Box 398166, Minneapolis, Minnesota 55439. Copyright © 2025 by Abdo Consulting Group, Inc. International copyrights reserved in all countries. No part of this book may be reproduced in any form without written permission from the publisher. Essential Library™ is a trademark and logo of Abdo Publishing.

Printed in China.
102024
012025

Cover Photo: Shutterstock Images (front); Nataly Studio/Shutterstock Images (back)
Interior Photos: Shutterstock Images, 1, 85; Atikan Pornchaiprasit/Shutterstock Images, 5; Everett Collection Historical/Alamy, 8; Bettmann/Getty Images, 11, 23; Ken Welsh/UCG/Universal Images Group/Getty Images, 15; Fort Worth Star-Telegram/Tribune News Service/Getty Images, 17; Duke Downey/San Francisco Chronicle/AP Images, 21; Vitaly Armand/AFP/Getty Images, 27; CFOTO/Future Publishing/Getty Images, 30; Arun Sankar/AFP/Getty Images, 34; Yuichi Yamazaki/Getty Images, 38; Fir Mamat/Alamy, 41; Chris Ratcliffe/Bloomberg/Getty Images, 43; Peter Power/Toronto Star/Getty Images, 47; Gene J. Puskar/AP Images, 49; Jeff Kravitz/FilmMagic, Inc/Getty Images, 53; New Africa/Shutterstock Images, 56–57; Red Line Editorial, 59; Tim Boyle/Getty Images, 62–63; ARS/Getty Images, 67; Daniel Acker/Bloomberg/Getty Images, 70; Thierry Monasse/Getty Images, 73; Allen J. Schaben/Los Angeles Times/Getty Images, 76–77; Scott Olson/Getty Images, 79; Jeffrey Greenberg/Universal Images Group/Getty Images, 82; Damian Dovarganes/AP Images, 87; AaronP/Bauer-Griffin/GC Images/Getty Images, 89; David Paul Morris/Bloomberg/Getty Images, 92; Anthony Wallace/AFP/Getty Images, 96

Editor: Arnold Ringstad
Series Designer: Maggie Villaume

Library of Congress Control Number: 2024938300

PUBLISHER'S CATALOGING-IN-PUBLICATION DATA

Names: Sonneborn, Liz, author.
Title: The fast food industry / by Liz Sonneborn
Description: Minneapolis, Minnesota: ABDO Publishing, 2025 | Series: Fascinating food | Includes online resources and index.
Identifiers: ISBN 9781098295240 (lib. bdg.) | ISBN 9798384916246 (ebook)
Subjects: LCSH: Fast foods--Juvenile literature. | Prepared food--Juvenile literature. | Convenience foods--Juvenile literature. | Fried food--Juvenile literature. | Food industry and trade--Juvenile literature. | Food service--Juvenile literature. | Fast food restaurants--Juvenile literature.
Classification: DDC 338.76164--dc23

CONTENTS

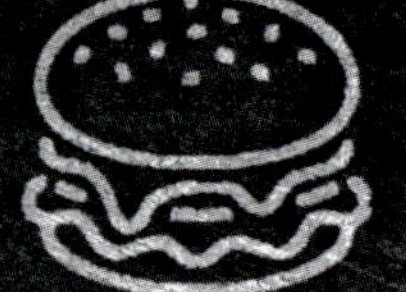

FAST, CHEAP, AND TASTY

In the late 1940s, anyone driving by the California restaurant owned by Dick and Mac McDonald would assume the brothers were thrilled with their thriving business. It was located in San Bernardino, then a sleepy town about 60 miles (97 km) east of Los Angeles. Every day, its parking lot was full of cars and teeming with customers eager to taste the restaurant's signature smoked barbecue and dozens of other menu items.

McDonald's was a drive-in, a popular type of restaurant at the time. After diners parked their cars, young female carhops offered them menus and took their orders. The carhops brought the orders to the kitchen and later delivered the food on trays. The customers ate in their cars.

Despite the restaurant's success, the McDonald brothers became tired of running it. They had

McDonald's, which began as a small local restaurant more than 80 years ago, eventually spread around the world and helped define the concept of fast food.

trouble hiring and keeping skilled cooks. The United States was experiencing an economic boom, so cooks had no trouble finding better-paying jobs. The carhops worked for tips, which meant they were more interested in chatting with the customers than in delivering food quickly.

The carhops also attracted groups of young men who often did not order any food. The rowdy crowds frequently broke dishes and stole silverware. Worst of all, although they were selling plenty of food, the McDonalds were not making the profits they wanted. This was largely because almost 40 percent of their revenue went to paying employees.[1]

THE SPEEDEE SERVICE SYSTEM

Dick and Mac finally decided to close the restaurant and start over. They wanted to find a way to sell more food with the fewest employees possible. To make orders simpler to fulfill, they drastically trimmed their menu. Hamburgers and cheeseburgers had made up 80 percent of their sales, so they kept only the burgers and a few other items such as french fries, milkshakes, and soda.[2]

The McDonalds then bought two huge custom-made six-foot (1.8 m) grills so workers could cook many burgers at once.[3] They also redesigned the kitchen to function like a factory assembly line with employees at various stations, each responsible for performing only one task. For instance, one worker cooked the burger, another added the condiments, and a third wrapped it up in paper. The system was efficient and made it easier to hire workers at low pay because each employee had to be trained to do just one simple thing.

The McDonalds decided to eliminate the carhops altogether. Instead, their new restaurant had windows where customers could place their orders. When the orders were ready, diners took the food back to their cars themselves. In essence, the system made the customers do the work the carhops had been doing before. The McDonald brothers also got rid of plates. Their burgers and fries now came in paper wrappers and cartons that could be thrown away. There was no need for utensils to eat these handheld foods.

POTATOES IN THE FRENCH MANNER

French fries have long been a favorite of fast food fans. But few know that Thomas Jefferson, the third president of the United States, introduced them to the nation. He had lived in Paris while serving as the ambassador to France. Jefferson instructed White House chef Honoré Julien to prepare potatoes "deep-fried while raw, in small cuttings, served in the French manner."[4]

The menu at the original McDonald's was far simpler than those at most modern fast food restaurants, which often list dozens of items.

Their customers quickly got used to McDonald's new restaurant operation, which the brothers called the Speedee Service System. They had slashed labor costs so low that they could afford to sell their hamburgers for only 15 cents. This was half the price of the same burger served in a typical diner.[5]

The new restaurant was an immediate success. In 1951, the McDonalds earned a profit of $100,000.[6] This is about $1.2 million in 2024 dollars.[7] Word about their restaurant spread throughout the food industry. In July 1952, *American Restaurant* magazine published a cover story on McDonald's. Its headline hailed that the restaurant sold "One Million Hamburgers and 160 Tons of French Fries a Year."[8]

THE McDONALD'S EMPIRE

Among those interested in the Speedee Service System was a middle-aged milkshake machine salesman named Ray Kroc. In his office in Chicago, Illinois, he began getting calls from restaurant owners eager to buy his company's Multimixers because they were used by McDonald's. Curious, Kroc looked up the McDonald's mixer order. He was stunned that a single restaurant had ordered eight Multimixers. Why, he wondered, did McDonald's need enough mixers to make 40 milkshakes at one time?[9]

During a business trip to Los Angeles, Kroc decided to find out for himself. One morning, he drove to San Bernardino, arriving at McDonald's at 10:00 a.m., about an hour before it opened. The restaurant was not very impressive. It looked like plenty of other drive-ins he had seen. Soon a crew of young men arrived, all dressed

FAST FOOD AND CALIFORNIA

Like McDonald's, many popular fast food chains—including Taco Bell, Carl's Jr., Jack in the Box, Panda Express, and Del Taco—got their start in California. It is not surprising that Californians were quick to embrace fast food. Beginning in the early 1900s, California's culture and development revolved around traveling by car. Fast food proved an ideal cuisine for a population that spent much of its time on roads and highways.

in crisp white shirts, pants, and paper hats. They carried large cartons of meat and buns and big sacks of potatoes inside. He later recalled that as they prepared to open the doors, "they were bustling around like ants at a picnic."[10]

By 11:00, customers were flooding the parking lot, and a long line formed. As Kroc took a place in it, he asked the man in front of him what the big deal was with this restaurant. The man, who was a regular customer, explained, "You'll get the best hamburger you ever ate for 15 cents. And you don't have to wait and mess around tipping waitresses."[11] With decades in the restaurant industry, Kroc immediately realized that the McDonald brothers had cracked a very lucrative code—how to sell tasty food to customers quickly at a low price.

That afternoon, he introduced himself to the McDonalds, who were excited to meet Mr. Multimixer, as they called him. They talked about the business and took him to meet their architect. He was designing a new style of McDonald's restaurant. It was to have two golden arches 30 feet (9 m) tall rising from the roof so that drivers could recognize the restaurant from far away.[12] That night, Kroc imagined hundreds of golden arches across the country. He was sure the McDonalds' formula could draw in customers anywhere.

He also thought about how
many Multimixers he could sell
to all those McDonald's locations.

Kroc pitched the McDonald
brothers his idea. To his surprise,
they were not interested. Mac
pointed to a large white house
on a hill near their restaurant.
He explained that their families
lived a happy life there. They
had no interest in spending all
their time traveling around the
country, overseeing the opening
of new restaurants.

Kroc, though, could think
of nothing he wanted to do
more. He negotiated to become
their franchise agent. He would
look for businesspeople who

While Kroc was not involved in the original creation of McDonald's, he became world-famous as the man who turned it into a gigantic, successful business.

wanted to operate a restaurant using the McDonald's
model. In exchange for use of the name and concept, they
would pay the McDonald brothers an initial fee and a cut of
their profits.

INVENTING A GLOBAL INDUSTRY

Kroc himself became the first franchisee. In 1955, he established a McDonald's in Des Plaines, Illinois, near where he had lived as a child. His restaurant served as a model that he could show potential franchisees. From its operation, he proved how much money a single McDonald's could generate.

In just five years, 228 McDonald's restaurants were operating in the United States.[13] Kroc wanted to keep opening more, but he grew weary of dealing with the McDonalds, who were slow in making decisions. In 1961, Kroc took over sole control of the business, buying the McDonald brothers out for $1 million each after taxes.[14]

Refining the model with new innovations, Kroc continued to grow the McDonald's empire until he died in 1984. By 2022 there were 40,275 McDonald's restaurants located in more than 100 countries.[15] But the McDonalds and Kroc did not just create a restaurant chain. They helped invent an entire industry—one devoted to providing customers with what has become known the world over as fast food.

Although it was not the first fast food restaurant, McDonald's popularized the basic business model followed by many other major fast food chains, including Burger King, Kentucky Fried Chicken, Pizza Hut, and Taco Bell. Fast food is generally food that is prepared quickly using efficient means and sold at a cheap price at restaurants, stands, and convenience stores. In addition to hamburgers and fries, common fast foods include hot dogs, tacos, burritos, sandwiches, and salads. Originally considered uniquely American, fast food is now a global phenomenon. Today, there are an estimated one million fast food outlets on Earth.[16]

CHAPTER TWO

ON THE GO

On a busy city street, a storefront with a counter covered in freshly prepared food beckons hungry passersby. Attracted by the colorful paintings adorning the store and by the luscious smells, potential customers stop to check out what dishes are for sale that day. If something appeals to them, they pay the proprietor and set off to enjoy their meal.

This scene played out in the city of Pompeii in what is now Italy almost 2,000 years ago. In 79 CE, Pompeii was destroyed when the volcano Mount Vesuvius erupted nearby. Covered in ash and rock, the city's preserved remains have been excavated by archaeologists since the 1700s. They have found about 80 *thermopolia*, or snack bars.[1]

The residents of Pompeii were not the only ancient people to consume prepared food on the go. Evidence of street vendors selling food has also

Visitors to Pompeii's thermopolia ate foods such as bread, cheese, goat, and duck.

been found at ancient sites in Asia. In ancient China, for instance, the poor often stopped at vendors selling blood soup at the end of a workday. Wealthier people sent their servants to purchase this delicious but cheap street food. Such archaeological finds reveal that preparing, eating, and enjoying fast food is a very old concept.

The United States also has a long history of fast food. Pushcarts serving fruit and sandwiches have been part of life in urban areas since the 1800s. Diners, cafeterias, and buffets also provided quick and cheap meals. By the early 1900s, restaurants called automats, which allowed customers to buy sandwiches, pie slices, and other foods from vending machines, were popular in cities. However, it wasn't until the 1920s that the first modern American fast food restaurant was born.

WHITE CASTLE

In 1916, a Kansas fry cook named Walt Anderson made a discovery. If he smashed small squares of ground beef on his griddle, he could cook numerous hamburgers quickly and evenly. He also found that if he put the burgers in buns instead of between slices of bread, the buns would soak up the grease, making his burgers easy to eat using one's hands.

With these innovations in mind, Anderson set up a three-stool hamburger stand outside a factory. At the time, hamburgers were considered a food for the working class. But some people were wary of hamburgers because the beef was sometimes mixed with other cheaper ingredients. To ease their concern, Anderson set up his meat grinder by his grill so customers could see there was no filler in his little 5-cent burgers. By delivering a high-quality hamburger quickly and cheaply, Anderson's stand proved a success, and he soon opened two more.

While preparing to open his fourth stand in 1921, Anderson met local real estate broker and entrepreneur Billy Ingram. Ingram admired Anderson's operation, but he did not think the fry cook was ambitious enough. Envisioning a chain of restaurants selling Anderson's hamburgers, Ingram persuaded the cook to take him on as a partner.

White Castle began with a $700 investment from Walt Anderson. Today the company earns hundreds of millions of dollars annually.

Ingram named their chain White Castle because, in a time before restaurant health regulations, it suggested to the customer that their restaurants were clean. For the same purpose, he created a standard design for the restaurants with white walls and gleaming stainless-steel counters. Ingram wanted to deliver a consistent experience and product in every White Castle.

All the restaurants looked the same, and cooks were trained to prepare food in a specific manner. That consistency became an important selling point. A 1932 brochure for the chain promised, "When you sit in a White Castle, remember that you are one of several thousands; you are sitting on the same kind of stool; you are being served on the same kind of counter . . . the hamburger you eat is prepared in exactly the same way over a gas flame of the same intensity."[2]

WIMPY

"I'll gladly pay you Tuesday for a hamburger today."[3] This promise was the famous catchphrase of J. Wellington Wimpy, a character who premiered in the *Thimble Theatre* cartoon strip in the 1930s. The hamburger-obsessed Wimpy was constantly trying to con someone into giving him his favorite meal for free. Wimpy's popularity reflected Americans' embrace of the hamburger during the Great Depression. He also inspired the Wimpy fast food chain, which operated in the United States from 1934 to 1977.

Ingram bought out Anderson in 1933. He expanded the White Castle chain first throughout the Midwest and South and then into the northeastern United States. By 1935, White Castle was selling 40 million hamburgers a year.[4]

Ingram was a clever entrepreneur, but much of White Castle's success was because of good timing. As the chain spread in the 1930s, its 5-cent burgers seemed like an especially good deal during the Great Depression, a severe economic downturn that left many Americans without jobs. Even people who were struggling financially could afford to occasionally treat themselves to White Castle.

White Castle also expanded just as more workers were moving from farms to cities to take jobs in factories and offices. These busy workers became a reliable customer base for the restaurants. In addition, agriculture was becoming industrialized in the United States during this era. As a result, prices for beef and wheat were dropping, allowing the restaurant chain to buy these ingredients at a low cost.

NEW CHAINS EMERGE

Other businesspeople took note of White Castle's success. Copycat chains, such as White Tower and White Palace, began popping up across the country. Other fast food outlets also appeared, many of which specialized in one type of food, such as hot dogs, coffee, or ice cream. One of the most popular was founded by Roy Allen and Frank Wright. Beginning in 1924, they oversaw a chain of A&W root beer stands by providing franchisees with use of their logo and their exclusive root beer syrup.

The ability of new chains to grow was curtailed by economic hardship in the 1930s and food rationing during World War II (1939–1945). Following the war, however, economic and social conditions were ideal for the growth of the fast food industry. The postwar boom raised the average worker's wage significantly, allowing many more people to afford consumer goods and restaurant meals.

The average American's growing wealth also made automobiles more affordable. Between 1945 and 1950, the yearly sales of new cars in the United States rose from 70,000 to 6.7 million.[5] Ready access to cars and the construction of the interstate highway system in the 1950s meant that Americans were on the move more than ever. As people drove along highways, fast food restaurants became a common source of meals for travelers and tourists.

The highway system also allowed many Americans to move from crowded city centers to newly constructed

neighborhoods in the suburbs. A baby boom among
postwar suburbanites also fueled the growth of the fast food
industry. As Kroc and other fast food pioneers recognized,
family-friendly restaurants
provided a valuable service to
young suburban parents by
giving them an economical and
easy way to feed themselves and
their children.

The car culture of the
postwar era also led to the
creation of the drive-through,
a successor to earlier drive-in
restaurants. Customers could
now order food, pay, and take
their meals home without

American car culture and the development of the interstate highway system helped spur the growth of the fast food industry.

ever leaving their cars. Several restaurants claim to have
created the drive-through, but its modern form using a
two-way speaker dates to 1948, when such a system was
implemented by In-N-Out Burger in California.

Because of the high demand for fast food, many chains
that are familiar today were established in the 1940s and
the 1950s. Founded by restaurant and motel owner Harland

Sanders in 1954, Kentucky Fried Chicken offered traditional Southern food such as coleslaw and biscuits and gravy in addition to its signature chicken. Insta-Burger King, later called Burger King, took Miami, Florida, by storm in 1957 with its supersized Whopper hamburger. Other chains that emerged during this period included Jack in the Box, Dunkin' Donuts (now called Dunkin'), Pizza Hut, and Domino's Pizza. In addition to the chains that remain household names today, many other fast food businesses failed, were sold to more successful companies, or remained local restaurants that never tried to go national.

GOING CORPORATE

In the early years of the fast food industry, visionary entrepreneurs often founded and ran popular chains. But beginning in the mid-1960s, many began selling their businesses to large corporations. To secure higher profits, these companies began to make changes in their operations. For instance, corporations often started using

COLONEL SANDERS

At an age when most people are planning to retire, Harland Sanders started a new business that became Kentucky Fried Chicken, one of the largest fast food chains in the world. Born on September 9, 1890, Sanders learned to cook as a child while caring for two younger siblings as his widowed mother worked. He opened Sanders Café in Corbin, Kentucky, in 1929. There he served Southern favorites such as biscuits, okra, and fried chicken, seasoned with his own recipe of eleven herbs and spices. In 1935, the governor of Kentucky gave the restaurateur the honorary title of colonel.

In 1956, at age 66, Sanders sold his business and began to franchise his method of cooking fried chicken. A born salesman, Sanders oversaw the establishment of 600 Kentucky Fried Chicken locations in seven years. He sold the chain in 1964 for $2 million but stayed on as the company spokesman.[7]

Wearing a white suit and black string tie, he appeared in commercials for the chain, and his image appeared on its packaging. A 1976 survey found that Colonel Sanders was the second most recognizable celebrity in the world. He remained in the public eye until his death in 1980. At the time, the Kentucky Fried Chicken empire had sales of $2 billion annually.[8]

LOVIE YANCEY AND FATBURGER

In 1947, the trailblazing Black entrepreneur Lovie Yancey and her husband opened Mr. Fatburger, a small hamburger stand in Los Angeles. After the couple parted ways five years later, she expanded the business and renamed it Fatburger. It eventually opened more than 200 locations.[9] In addition to big burgers and thick fries, Yancey's restaurants were known for their jukeboxes, which constantly blared lively music. Over the years, Fatburger attracted many celebrity fans, including basketball star Earvin "Magic" Johnson and actress and rapper Queen Latifah.

cheaper ingredients and adding artificial flavors and preservatives.

Corporations wanting to expand their chains ran into a problem. Suburban neighborhoods, highway hubs, and small towns were oversaturated with fast food outlets. To find a new market, they began building restaurants in urban areas.

Unlike in the suburbs, outlets in city centers did not require much, if any, parking. But they did need larger dining rooms to accommodate foot traffic. Many chains added dining rooms to their other locations as well. In many communities, fast food dining rooms became what sociologists call third places—places outside of homes and workplaces where people can gather informally.

Initially, most urban franchise owners were white. But fast food corporations, hoping to foster goodwill from

more diverse populations in cities, began to recruit people
of color to own restaurants, often with the help of loans
from the federal government. But some communities did
not welcome fast food outlets, because much of the profit
they generated benefited faraway corporate offices and
shareholders rather than the community itself. Still, fast
food restaurants did offer employment for local workers
and provided for many communities a treasured third place that anyone could access for the price of a coffee or soda.

By the late 1900s, urban markets themselves became oversaturated. American fast food corporations, however, still wanted to expand. Again, they had to look for new markets—this time, far from home.

CHAPTER THREE

CONQUERING THE WORLD

On January 31, 1990, eager customers started lining up in the early morning despite bitterly cold winter weather. They were excited to eat at the first McDonald's ever to open in Russia, which was part of the Soviet Union then. The huge fast food joint in the center of the capital city of Moscow was, at the time, the largest McDonald's in the world, boasting 27 cash registers and 900 seats.[1]

That day, the Moscow McDonald's saw large crowds. Most customers seemed confused but delighted by the unfamiliar American food on the menu, despite its high price. A Big Mac, french fries, and a drink cost about half a day's wage for the average worker. Many diners were also surprised by the behavior of the staff, who had been schooled in American-style service. Soviets were not accustomed

The first McDonald's in Moscow served about 30,000 people on its opening day.

to smiling staff members asking "May I help you?" and
saying "Thank you for coming."

The opening of the restaurant made international news.
At the time, the United States and the Soviet Union were
bitter enemies. The Soviets had long condemned American
society as decadent. People around the world were
therefore surprised that so many customers in Moscow
would enthusiastically embrace McDonald's. The
company was by then seen as so deeply American that it
had become a symbol of the United States itself.

Today, the success of the first Moscow McDonald's
seems less puzzling. Since its opening, American fast
food chains have made footholds in nations throughout the world. The appeal of
fast food has proven nearly universal. Even in countries that
are very different socially, culturally, and politically from the

United States, fast food is one part of the American way of life that has been widely accepted.

NEW MARKETS

The American fast food industry made its first forays into the international market in the late 1950s. Chains mostly established outlets in English-speaking countries or in nations where the US Army had military bases. By 1975, there were more than 2,000 American fast food restaurants outside the United States.[2]

Most of these were found in Canada, Australia, Japan, and various nations in Europe, all of which had strong economies. This ensured there were enough customers with disposable income to spend on fast food. Like many Americans, these middle-class customers were able and willing to pay for a quick and convenient meal.

In the late 1900s, chains looked to expand into China, the world's most populous country. A pioneer in this project, McDonald's opened its first restaurant in Hong Kong in 1975. It quickly proved popular with young people, who found the food exotic and modern. Its success led McDonald's to establish outlets in mainland China. By 1992, China had seven of the ten largest McDonald's restaurants in the world.

In 2023, KFC opened its 10,000th Chinese location.

Kentucky Fried Chicken, later renamed KFC, also was aggressive in entering the Chinese market. In 1987, it opened its largest restaurant in the Chinese capital of Beijing.

In the 1990s and 2000s, chains moved into Southeast Asia, Latin America, India, and Africa. With incomes rising in these areas, corporations hoped to find new customers. Fast food companies had become confident that they could adapt to appeal to people in any culture.

DOING BUSINESS ABROAD

Still, fast food chains have encountered many challenges when they have tried to establish themselves in a new country. One problem is dealing with different legal and economic systems. For many companies, the best solution for overcoming this hurdle is the franchise business model, in which individual outlets are small, locally owned businesses. Owners familiar with the area often have personal relationships with bankers and food suppliers who can help them open and run their business. Generally, chains want non-American outlets to buy their ingredients locally, although in some places that is difficult because the meat of local breeds of cattle and chickens may not taste the same as their American counterparts.

Local businesspeople are also likely to understand the unstated business customs of a country. For instance, in some countries, corrupt officials may expect bribes to issue necessary permits. A chain's parent company usually does not want to get involved with such deals. It may prefer to turn a blind eye while local franchise owners do what is necessary to run their business.

Even in countries hostile to the United States, officials often support fast food franchises. The franchise system allows local businesspeople to prosper. It also helps the overall economy by introducing the country to new technologies and business practices.

TASTY AND THAT'S IT

Politics sometimes interferes with the operations of American fast food chains abroad. For example, McDonald's was pressured to close 850 restaurants in Russia in March 2022.[3] Russia had invaded Ukraine, and many US corporations pulled out of the country in protest. The McDonald's locations soon reopened under the name Vkusno i tochka, meaning "tasty and that's it." The new chain made its own versions of McDonald's classic menu items, among them the Big Hit—a double-pattied burger much like the Big Mac, but with its own special sauce.

Knowledge of the industry acquired by franchisees helps foreign businesspeople start their own homegrown fast food chains, including Pret A Manger in the United Kingdom, Paris Baguette in South Korea, El Pollo Loco in Mexico, and Nando's in South Africa. One of the earliest was MOS Burger, which was established in Japan in 1972, one year after the first McDonald's opened in that country. Its owners studied the McDonald's operation not to copy it, but to avoid its mistakes. Rather than touting its cheap prices and speed at filling orders, MOS Burger instead emphasized the quality of its ingredients.

TWEAKING THE MENU

American fast food restaurants operating abroad generally try to replicate the menu items served in the United States.

But many chains discovered they needed to change their offerings to suit local tastes. For instance, Dunkin' initially struggled to connect with Indian customers, who were unfamiliar with the flavors in its donuts. The chain found success only after it introduced popular flavors used in Indian sweets, such as saffron, pistachio, and almond.

Chains often keep their core menu but add a few items that have local appeal. McDonald's has offered McLaks (a grilled salmon sandwich) in Norway, McPepper (a burger with black pepper sauce) in Singapore, and McZuri (a veal burger with hash browns and mushroom sauce) in Switzerland. In India, Pizza Hut has served Birizza, a take on the popular Indian dish biryani. Birizza was topped with seasoned rice, meat, and vegetables, covered with a second pizza crust, and served with gravy. Some fast food restaurants also serve alcohol because of popular demand. In Germany, beer

FAST FOOD IN JAPAN

The menus of fast food restaurants outside of the United States often feature items not seen in US locations. Some of the most inventive have popped up in Japan. Burger Kings there have sold the NY Pizza Burger, which was the size of a small pizza. The Mega Tamago at McDonald's in Japan had double the meat of a Big Mac plus an egg patty and bacon. The beef patty in the Surf and Turf Burger at Japanese Wendy's restaurants was topped with lobster meat.

Burger King locations in India offer unique local menu options, such as the Paneer Royale Wrap.

is often on the menu, while in France, wine is sometimes featured. At a McDonald's in Rio de Janeiro, Brazil, waiters pour glasses of champagne while customers eat their Big Macs by candlelight.

Fast food operations also alter their menus to conform to religious dietary restrictions. In Israel, Burger King, KFC, Sbarro, and other chains serve kosher food, which is prepared according to Jewish law. In countries with large Muslim populations, restaurants serve only meats certified as halal, which requires that animals be slaughtered in a certain way as detailed in Muslim religious law.

Because Hindus in India consider cows sacred and do not eat beef, fast food outlets offer vegetarian burgers, such as McDonald's McAloo Tikki burger, which features a patty made from potatoes and peas.

THE SLOW FOOD MOVEMENT

Despite the American fast food industry's efforts to cater to international customers, local populations sometimes oppose having fast food restaurants in their communities. Possibly the most dramatic resistance occurred in Rome, Italy, in 1986, when the country's first McDonald's opened at the Piazza di Spagna. Thousands of protesters gathered outside, demanding the city shut the restaurant down. They complained that the McDonald's was degrading a historic center and causing traffic congestion. They said the crowd outside the restaurant was too loud and the smell of fried food was nauseating.

The protesters spoke out against fast food as unhealthful. And perhaps most important to a people proud of their culinary heritage, they also condemned the "Americanization" of the national palate. During the protest, journalist Carlo Petrini served supporters plates of pasta to remind them of the glories of Italian cuisine.

The protest had some lasting effects. Petrini founded the Slow Food Movement, which now has organizations in more than 160 countries, including the United States.[4] In addition to speaking about the health risks fast food poses, the movement promotes good nutrition and seeks to preserve local food traditions around the world. The movement, however, has done little to slow the growth of the fast food industry internationally.

A GLOBAL CUISINE

Fast food became a global phenomenon for a simple reason: international customers are eager to buy it. They embrace fast food for many of the reasons Americans do. It is a cheap, quick, and easy way to have a meal. In countries with emerging economies that have been most recently targeted by the fast food industry, workers' incomes are rising, allowing them to afford to eat out. American-style fast food, however, is also an appealing novelty. In places where people previously had access only to local foods that had been

By 2022, about 67 percent of the fast food industry's revenue came from restaurants outside the United States.[5]

traditionally cooked in a certain way, fast food can seem new and exciting.

In some countries, a visit to a fast food restaurant became a special event. For instance, in China during the 1990s, tourists in Beijing often made a point of going to McDonald's or KFC. Fast food costs more than traditional street food, so going to these restaurants seemed like a luxury. When customers traveled home, they brought back fast food containers and paper cups as souvenirs to impress their friends and family.

In many places, fast food quickly became a part of the local culture. Japan even created an annual tradition known as Kentucky Christmas. It came into being in 1974 after the owner of Japan's first Kentucky Fried Chicken franchise learned that Americans living in Japan came to his store for Christmas dinner because they could not buy a turkey. With his encouragement, the chain launched a national campaign called Kurisumasu ni wa Kentakkii!, meaning "Kentucky for Christmas."

The promotion was a massive success. Now, each year, the company makes Christmas-themed buckets, and stores decorate Colonel Sanders statues with Santa hats and wreaths. Only about 1 percent of people in Japan actually

KFC is such a popular Christmas tradition in Japan that restaurants begin taking reservations for the meals as early as October.

celebrate Christmas, but millions of families feast on fried chicken every December 25.[6]

When chains first went international, fast food was seen as distinctly American. As symbols of the United States, fast food restaurants in foreign cities were sometimes bombed by terrorists with grievances against the US government. But as other cultures have become accustomed to fast food, it has come to seem less American and more part of an international culture. A sign written in English in a KFC in Phnom Penh, Cambodia, made this point by assuring customers the restaurant would provide them with "the same taste enjoyed in Sydney, Kuala Lumpur, and Portland, Oregon."[7] Despite its distinctly American origins, fast food has emerged as the first truly global culinary tradition.

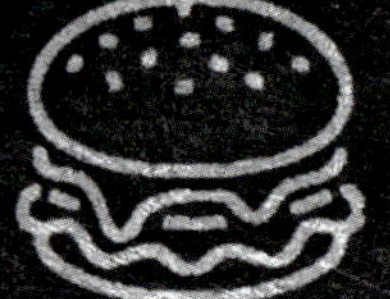

CHAPTER FOUR

KEEPING CUSTOMERS HAPPY

Lou Groen was an early McDonald's franchisee. He started operating his first location in Cincinnati, Ohio, in 1959. Soon after opening its doors, he was in a panic. His McDonald's took in only about $300 a day, which, after his expenses, left him with meager profits. But what really alarmed him was his average Friday take, which amounted to a dismal $75.[1]

Groen knew exactly what the problem was. About 87 percent of the people living in the surrounding neighborhood were Catholic.[2] At the time, the Catholic Church forbade its congregants from eating meat on Friday, so his most reliable customers avoided burgers on that day. Knowing that the church allowed fish on Fridays, Groen came up with a plan. He decided that he would persuade McDonald's head Ray Kroc to let him sell a new menu item—a fish sandwich.

The McDonald's Filet-O-Fish, which is still offered today, is made from Alaskan pollock.

Groen experimented with several recipes before coming up with a sandwich filled with a battered filet of haddock topped by a slice of cheese. In 1961, he presented his creation to Kroc, who disliked it, declaring, "I don't want my stores stunk up with the smell of fish."[3] But Kroc suspected that Groen was right that there was a market for a beefless burger. In fact, he had already come up with his own—the Hula Burger, which replaced the beef patty with a slice of pineapple.

On Good Friday in 1962, Kroc decided to test the two new burger creations in a head-to-head match. In several stores, Groen's fish sandwich was placed on the menu alongside Kroc's Hula Burger. The contest wasn't even close. The fish sandwich won hands down, selling 350 orders against the Hula Burger's dismal six. Kroc, realizing he had a new hit menu item, conceded defeat. By 1965, the Filet-O-Fish, marketed as "the fish that catches people," was on sale at McDonald's restaurants throughout the country. By 2013, the chain was selling about 300 million of the sandwiches each year.[4]

INTRODUCING NEW MENU ITEMS

The invention of the Filet-O-Fish was an early example of a fast food chain hitting it big with a new item, but it was far

from the last. To stay competitive, chains have constantly worked to revamp their menus. Sometimes, as in the case of the Filet-O-Fish, they add new items because of customer demand. Other times, chains with a steady eye on their competitors adopt copycat versions of successful foods sold by other restaurants.

One of the most industry-changing menu items was Burger King's Whopper, which the chain introduced in 1957. Cofounder Jim McLamore created the sandwich after realizing that the Texas chain Whataburger was doing well by selling a large burger. As the name suggested, McLamore's Whopper was much bigger than burgers sold by most other chains. Its beef patty weighed in at four ounces (113 g), more than twice the size of a McDonald's burger at the time.[5] To compete with Burger King, McDonald's invented its own large burger, the Big Mac, in 1968. Since then, large burgers have become the norm at most fast food chains.

The introduction of a food item can also open up entirely new markets for chains. McDonald's was considering selling breakfast when in 1971 franchisee Herb Peterson from Santa Barbara, California, came up with a new fast food breakfast product—the Egg McMuffin. Peterson was motivated by his love of eggs Benedict, an elegant breakfast dish made from poached eggs and ham or Canadian bacon placed on English muffin slices and topped with hollandaise sauce.

Because of the gooey eggs and dripping sauce, a traditional eggs Benedict must be eaten with a knife and fork. To make a version that could be eaten with one's hands,

Peterson turned eggs Benedict into a sandwich with English muffins at the top and bottom. He replaced the hollandaise with cheese and the poached egg with a slice of egg cooked in a metal ring. The Egg McMuffin's successful rollout in 1975 inspired McDonald's to create an entire breakfast menu two years later.

FOR A LIMITED TIME

Often chains offer new foods on a limited-time basis. This strategy caters to many customers' desire for novelty. It also allows chains to test an item's popularity before giving it a permanent place on the menu. One of the most successful limited-time offers is the McDonald's McRib, a pork sandwich slathered with barbecue sauce that debuted in 1981 and has been on and off the chain's regular menu ever since. Because of its loyal fans, each revival and retirement has been greeted with great fanfare in the press.

Some promotions seem designed more to attract media attention than to appeal to customers' appetites. In 2014, for instance, Arby's rolled out its notorious Meat Mountain. The concoction, true to its name, featured a heap of sliced turkey, ham, corned beef, Angus steak, and roast beef, along with chicken tenders, Swiss and cheddar cheeses, and bacon.

Another way fast food restaurants tweak their menus to keep customers coming back is by offering value menus featuring items sold at a discount price. Wendy's pioneered the value menu in 1989, during a period when other burger chains were trying to undercut one another by selling signature items such as Whoppers and Big Macs for 99 cents. Wendy's upped the ante by offering a special menu of nine 99-cent items, including hamburgers, french fries, and soft drinks, allowing customers to assemble a full meal for just a few dollars.

Chains also encourage customers to order more food by bundling items at a lower price than if they were sold individually. Usually such value meals include a sandwich or entrée with fries or another side dish and a drink. Value meals are often assigned a number for easy ordering, making it possible for customers to order full meals without much thought.

MARKETING TO KIDS

In addition to enticing customers with new menu items and low prices, fast food chains compete with one another through marketing. Each chain's marketing campaigns and advertisements tout special qualities and experiences

DAVE THOMAS

The founder of Wendy's, Dave Thomas, became a beloved television personality by appearing in hundreds of commercials for his fast food chain. Born in 1932, Thomas was the manager of a barbecue restaurant in Fort Wayne, Indiana, when he became friends with Harland Sanders, the founder of Kentucky Fried Chicken. In 1962, Thomas began managing four low-earning Kentucky Fried Chicken restaurants in Columbus, Ohio. Thomas quickly turned the fortunes of these locations around.

Thomas used the money from this success to open his own restaurant in Columbus, naming it Wendy's after the nickname of one of his daughters. Through franchising, he built a chain that eventually grew to more than 6,000 outlets.[7] In 1989, an advertising executive suggested he become the Wendy's pitchman. Wearing a white short-sleeved shirt and a red tie, Thomas displayed a folksy yet charismatic presence in the ads that caught on with the American public.

Thomas used his celebrity to promote adoption, which, as an adoptee, was a cause close to his heart. He established the Dave Thomas Foundation for Adoption and worked with President Bill Clinton to pass legislation to aid adoptive parents. Respected for both his charitable work and his business savvy, Thomas died in 2002 at the age of 69.

customers can expect when visiting their restaurants. Much of the early marketing for fast food restaurants painted them as places where families could get a good and quick meal.

In 1963, a McDonald's franchisee in Washington, DC, began running ads on local television. To attract families, the advertisements directly appealed to children using a clown character named Ronald McDonald. In 1965, the first national television ad featuring Ronald McDonald aired, and in 1966 the clown character became the chain's official spokesman.

Seemingly endless television spots depicted a fantasy world called McDonaldland, where Ronald McDonald interacted with Mayor McCheese, the Hamburglar, and other colorful characters. By the early 1970s, 96 percent of all American children could recognize Ronald McDonald.[8] The only character with greater recognition was Santa Claus.

Fast food chains have long used playgrounds to attract children, but this practice has declined in recent decades due to health and safety concerns.

Other fast food chains soon followed McDonald's example by using brightly colored packaging and installing playgrounds outside their restaurants. Research showed that marketing to children was effective. When children asked their parents for fast food, parents agreed to get it about one-third of the time.[10] Chains also realized that if children became regular customers, they were likely to remain loyal to their family's favorite fast food brand for the rest of their lives.

FUN MEALS AND TIE-INS

In 1973 the now-defunct Burger Chef chain discovered a new way to entice young customers. Its menu offered the Fun Meal—the first fast food kid's meal to feature a colorful box with a burger, dessert, and toy inside. Other chains soon copied the innovation, most notably McDonald's, which introduced its own Happy Meal in 1978. Today, McDonald's sells so many Happy Meals that it is one of the biggest toy distributors in the world.

To appeal to the youth market, Burger Chef also pioneered promotions linked to the release of a film or the premiere of a television show. In 1977, the chain gave away posters to promote the movie *Star Wars* and featured illustrations of the film's characters on Fun Meal trays. By the 1990s, movie fast food tie-ins had become more elaborate, with movie images appearing on cups, bags, posters, and in-restaurant displays. Often toy giveaways and menu items were associated with the promoted movie.

Fast food chains have also promoted their products within the institution most associated with children—

local schools. They sponsor sports teams and programs, often in exchange for the right to place advertising materials in school hallways and sports stadiums. A common way schools raise funds is to sell books of coupons for fast food. Some schools even sell branded fast food in their cafeterias.

In recent decades, the fast food industry has frequently come under fire for its relentless marketing to children. Parents and other concerned adults are upset that children are subject to manipulative marketing techniques. They are also worried about the health effects of fast food itself.

SZECHUAN SAUCE PROMOTION

In 2017, a promotion at a Los Angeles McDonald's got way out of hand. Months earlier, the animated show *Rick and Morty* aired an episode about a character's obsession with the Szechuan dipping sauce McDonald's offered in 1998 to promote the movie *Mulan*. The popularity prompted the company to bring the sauce back for a one-day promotional event. A big crowd gathered outside a Los Angeles location that said it had a supply. When the restaurant revealed it had only 20 packets, people became violent. The police had to be called to settle the crowd.

CHAPTER FIVE

NUTRITION WOES

Documentary filmmaker Morgan Spurlock decided to conduct an experiment with himself as the guinea pig. To challenge McDonald's claims that their food was nutritious, he decided to eat at McDonald's for breakfast, lunch, and dinner for 30 days, while limiting his physical activity. Spurlock enlisted three doctors and a nutritionist to monitor his health.

Spurlock had one more rule for his McDonald's experience. At the time, the chain offered "supersize" food items, which provided larger portions than the regular size for just a small increase in price. Anytime a McDonald's employee asked if he wanted to supersize his order, he had to say yes.

Once Spurlock plunged into his experiment, it did not take long before his health appeared to suffer.

Morgan Spurlock's 2004 documentary *Super Size Me* brought massive mainstream attention to the issue of fast food's health effects.

In 2018, the US Food and Drug Administration began requiring chain restaurants with 20 or more outlets to post the calorie counts of menu items.[2] Nutrition experts hoped that seeing calorie counts would discourage diners from ordering high-calorie foods. But most studies have found that posted calorie counts have little effect on people's ordering choices. Requiring restaurants to post calories might, however, have one positive public health effect. When restaurants add new items to their menu, they often try to lower the number of calories in them so that they will appeal to health-conscious customers.

He soon began to experience mood swings and depression. One of his doctors became so concerned over the condition of his liver that he asked Spurlock to stop before the 30 days were up. In the end, Spurlock finished his project. His cholesterol level had risen by 60 points.[1]

Spurlock recorded his experience in the 2004 documentary *Super Size Me*. Since its premiere, Spurlock's methodology has been questioned because of a 2018 confession that he had been heavily drinking alcohol on a regular basis for the previous 30 years, which appeared to include the time of the film's experiment. He had not disclosed this to the doctors during filming. But when *Super Size Me* first appeared, it caused a sensation. It forced many Americans to confront something most already knew but may have preferred to ignore. The fast food they loved was not a healthful dining option.

FAT, SALT, AND SUGAR

The nutritiousness of fast food has long been a subject of debate. In 1930, Billy Ingram, cofounder of White Castle, felt compelled to offer the public proof that his hamburgers were a healthful food. He enlisted a young medical school student to eat only White Castle hamburgers for three months, eating as many as 24 of them a day. In Ingram's account of the experiment, the student emerged from the ordeal in good health. His report concluded that "a normal healthy child could eat nothing but our hamburgers and water, and fully develop all its physical and mental faculties."[3]

Despite Ingram's assurances, critics continued to question the healthfulness of fast food, becoming especially vocal in the 1980s. While serving as the director of nutrition at the International Diabetes Center, nutrition expert Marion J. Franz published *Fast Food Facts* in 1983, which increased public concern about fast food products. The next year, nutritionist Bonnie Liebman of the Center for Science in the Public Interest raised the alarm about McDonald's french fries, which had high levels of cholesterol because they were fried in beef tallow. Two other people associated with the Center for Science in the Public Interest, Michael Jacobson

Nutritionists caution people against the overconsumption of unhealthy fast food options such as burgers, pizza, and fried foods.

and Sarah Fritschner, published *The Fast-Food Guide* in 1986. Their work popularized the phrase "empty calories," which they used to describe high-calorie fast food items that offered little nutritional value.[4]

Nutritionists have long pointed out that fast food offers few vegetables, fruits, or whole grains, which means that it lacks fiber and many important vitamins and minerals. They also note that fast food often contains a lot of fat, salt,

and sugar. These ingredients are cheap flavor enhancers that provide customers with the fatty, salty, and sweet tastes they crave.

Fast food chains also use artificial flavorings and chemical additives to make their food especially appealing. Chemists engineer fast food that gives the consumer the most pleasurable experience possible. Because of this, some critics of fast food argue that it is addictive.

BANNING BIG SODAS

In 2012, New York City mayor Michael Bloomberg placed a ban on the sale of sugary drinks larger than 16 ounces (0.5 L) as a public health measure.[6] Fast food industry executives were outraged by the ban, fearing other health-related regulations on their industry might follow. The public was also critical of the ban. A *New York Times* poll found that 60 percent of New Yorkers considered it a bad idea.[7] The ban was challenged in court and struck down in 2014, allowing the city's fast food restaurants to again serve giant sodas.

Even though McDonald's has long since abandoned supersizing, large portion sizes still come under fire. Discounted meal bundles encourage customers to buy more food than they might otherwise. While just about every item on fast food menus has gotten bigger over time, the growth of sugary soft drinks has been especially large. Originally, fast food restaurants offered eight-ounce (0.2 L) drinks. But because soda can be purchased at a low cost, chains have consistently increased soda portions to lure in customers. Soda cups now sometimes hold as much as 64 ounces (1.9 L), often with free refills.[5]

The amount of fat, salt, and sugar can also pose a danger to consumers' health. Trans fats can raise cholesterol levels, putting people at risk of heart disease. Salt can increase blood pressure, leaving people more vulnerable to heart

Fast Food Nutrition Facts

McDONALD'S BIG MAC[8]
590 calories
Total fat 34g .... **44% DV**
    Saturated fat 11g ....**56% DV**
Cholesterol 85 mg ....**28% DV**
Sodium 1050 mg ....**46% DV**

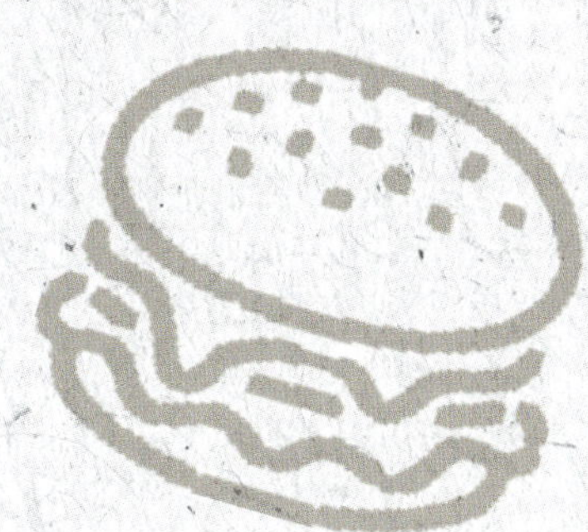

KFC'S CLASSIC CHICKEN SANDWICH[9]
650 calories
Total fat 35 g ....**54% DV**
    Saturated fat 4.5 g .....**23% DV**
Cholesterol 90 mg ....**30% DV**
Sodium 1260 mg ....**53% DV**

TACO BELL'S BLACK BEAN GRILLED CHEESE BURRITO[11]
700 calories
Total fat 37 g ....**47% DV**
    Saturated fat 15 g ....**75% DV**
Cholesterol 55 mg ....**18% DV**
Sodium 1390 mg ....**60% DV**

BURGER KING'S WHOPPER[10]
670 calories
Total fat 41 g ....**52% DV**
    Saturated fat 12 g ....**61% DV**
Cholesterol 85 mg ....**28% DV**
Sodium 1170 mg ....**51% DV**

Fast food chains often have nutrition information on their websites, including the number of calories and the amount of fat, cholesterol, and sodium (salt) in menu items. DV stands for "daily value" and indicates the percentage of the maximum recommended daily intake of nutrients based on a 2,000-calorie-a-day diet.

attacks, strokes, and kidney disease. The ingredients in fast food are also linked to increased inflammation, high cancer rates, and the development of memory disorders, such as Alzheimer's disease.

THE BACKLASH AGAINST FAST FOOD

In 2003, the families of two New York City teenagers took McDonald's to court. In *Pelman v. McDonald's Corporation,* they claimed that McDonald's bore responsibility for the teens' health issues because its deceptive advertising had not fully disclosed the health risks of eating the chain's food. A Manhattan judge threw out the case, stating, "Nobody is forced to eat at McDonald's."[12]

With the dismissal, the fast food industry breathed a sigh of relief, because, as the judge pointed out, a victory for the plaintiffs could have sparked a torrent of similar lawsuits. To prevent other such lawsuits against fast food chains, several state legislatures, under pressure from fast food lobbyists, passed so-called "cheeseburger laws" that forbade people from filing such lawsuits.[13]

Nevertheless, the threat of lawsuits along with the popularization of the idea that fast food is unhealthful led companies to make changes. One solution was to claim that they were not actually selling fast food. Some chains adopted new slogans to distance themselves from the fast food label. Dairy Queen declared it served "fan food, not fast food," referring to fans of the brand. Wendy's promised, "It's waaaay better than fast food." McDonald's assured customers that its products were "good food, served fast."[14] The entire industry gave itself a makeover by renaming fast food outlets to quick-service restaurants (QSR).

Chains also began changing their menus to give the impression of more healthful offerings. The strategy was far from new. In the 1980s and 1990s, fast food restaurants often tweaked their menus to provide lower-calorie versions of their foods. For instance, Pizza Hut offered a "light pizza" with

THE McLEAN DELUXE

In 1991, McDonald's debuted its McLean Deluxe burger. The burger had lower fat content than the chain's usual burgers. The chain was convinced it would appeal to health-conscious diners. But within two years, industry experts deemed it a flop, estimating it made up less than 2 percent of McDonald's sales.[15] The public turned on the McLean when it was reported that, to add moisture, the burger contained carrageenan. This food additive is made from seaweed, a fact that some consumers saw as unappetizing. By 1996, the McLean was off the McDonald's menu.

Chipotle, one of the most popular fast casual chains, has more than 3,500 locations around the world.

lower-calorie toppings, and Dairy Queen sold the Breeze, a Blizzard-like dessert made with yogurt instead of ice cream. In recent years, chains have tried to incorporate more healthful options into their menus, such as salads, fresh fruit, milk, and oatmeal. These items, however, have not always been as healthful as they might appear. For instance, many fast food salads have dressings packed with fat and sugar.

FAST CASUAL RESTAURANTS

Fast food restaurants have also been pressured to change by new competitors known as fast casual restaurants. As with fast food restaurants, customers place orders at a counter and seat themselves, and their food is delivered to them relatively quickly. Fast casual restaurant chains include Chipotle, Five Guys, Au Bon Pain, and Panera Bread.

However, fast casual food often costs about double the price of its fast food counterparts. Capitalizing on negative feelings toward fast food, some chains justify the higher prices by stressing that they use high-quality ingredients and more health-conscious recipes. In reality, though, many offerings at fast casual restaurants are high in calories, fat, and salt. In 2016, researchers at the University of South Carolina surveyed the menus of 62 restaurant chains and found that entrées at fast casual restaurants averaged 200 more calories than entrées at fast food outlets.[16]

Nevertheless, to compete with the fast casual industry, fast food chains have tried introducing what customers may perceive as more sophisticated fare. For example, McDonald's marketed the Artisan Grilled Chicken Sandwich and the Steakhouse Sirloin Third Pound Burger. Some fast food restaurants have also redesigned their interiors, adopting the more muted color schemes favored in the fast casual industry.

For decades, the fast food industry has tried to respond to public demands for more healthful food, but customers have largely rejected these efforts. Instead of ordering veggie burgers or grilled chicken sandwiches, they often default to their favorite quarter-pounder burgers, chicken nuggets, or french fries. For many people who grew up with fast food, it is considered a treat or an indulgence. They do not want health concerns to get in the way of what they see as the pleasure of a fast food meal.

CHAPTER SIX

HIDDEN HARMS

nvestigative journalist Eric Schlosser wrote the 2001 book *Fast Food Nation: The Dark Side of the All-American Meal* about the impact of the fast food industry on nearly every facet of American life. In its introduction, Schlosser wrote:

> *Fast food has proven to be a revolutionary force in American life. . . . During a relatively brief period of time, the fast food industry has helped to transform not only the American diet, but also our landscape, economy, workforce, and popular culture. Fast food and its consequences have become inescapable.*[1]

The best-selling book revealed the many ways fast food has negatively affected society—from creating dangerous workplaces to facilitating animal cruelty to damaging the environment. In the decades since its publication, many customers have

Technicians test cattle feces samples to detect disease in the animals. Tainted meat is among the issues that Eric Schlosser's books have highlighted.

demanded changes in the fast food industry to remedy the ills Schlosser outlined. Although the industry has initiated some reforms, food activists maintain it needs to do much more to address and end its most destructive practices.

FOOD PRODUCTION

The fast food industry purchases an enormous amount of food each year. McDonald's, for instance, is one of the biggest buyers of beef and potatoes in the world. With its massive buying power, the fast food industry has a major influence on how food is produced in the United States. Its goal of buying plant and animal products at the lowest possible cost has led to farming methods that activists argue are abusive to both workers and animals.

Fast food's demands for the increased production of meat, dairy, and eggs also transformed how livestock is raised in the United States. On factory farms, cows, chickens, and pigs live in facilities designed to produce a large quantity of animal products for the lowest price possible. Animals are often crowded together in cages and crates. To speed their growth, they are given artificial growth hormones.

Some activists have criticized these practices. To address such concerns, some fast casual chains have made their opposition to factory farming a selling point. Chipotle, for instance, calls its products "food with integrity" because it says it uses meat only from animals raised humanely.[2]

Fast food is often contaminated with industrial chemicals called phthalates, which are used to make plastic soft. Phthalates likely get into food when it comes in contact with food-moving conveyor belts or rubber gloves worn by workers. Ingested phthalates have been linked to attention and behavioral disorders.

To keep them water-repellent, fast food wrappers are often coated with perfluoroalkyl substances. Ingesting these chemicals has been linked to high cholesterol, immune disorders, and some cancers.

ENDANGERING THE PLANET

Some food activists take issue with not only the practices of meat production but also the environmental effects of producing the large quantities of animal products required

Each cow releases up to 264 pounds (120 kg) of methane per year.

by the fast food industry. One of these effects is related to

land use. Environmentalists have raised concerns about

links between the fast food industry and the destruction

of rainforests. Chains sometimes buy beef produced by

ranchers who have burned down sections of rainforests

in order to seed pastures to feed their cattle. Because

rainforests house about half of Earth's known species, losing

these ecosystems leads to a decrease in the diversity of plant

and animal life. Rainforests also absorb carbon dioxide in

the atmosphere, so their destruction worsens the effects of climate change.

Raising livestock itself is a significant contributor to climate change. Animal agriculture accounts for about 15 percent of greenhouse gas emissions.[3] Beef production is especially harmful, because cattle release methane into the atmosphere. To counter critics who condemn the fast food industry's role in climate change, Burger King announced in 2020 that it would sell a version of the Whopper made with meat from cows that had been fed lemongrass, which cuts their methane emissions.

FINDING SOLUTIONS

Several fast food chains have also been offering and promoting more plant-based burgers, which are promoted as avoiding the negative environmental effects of raising cattle. For instance, McDonald's began selling burgers made from the plant-based product Beyond Beef in select locations. Fast food restaurants' promotion of meat alternatives has helped consumers accept these new products. Between 2019 and 2020, the sales of these plant-based foods grew by 45 percent in the United States. However, they still amounted to only 1 percent of all meat products sold.[4] Critics note that these products are expensive, heavily processed, and not necessarily healthful.

Fast casual restaurants such as Panera Bread and Just Salad have begun to include notes on their menus indicating the impact individual products have on climate change. Fast food restaurants have not yet embraced this trend. A study from Johns Hopkins University's Bloomberg School of Public Health, however, found that labeling beef items as having "high climate impact" can have a significant effect on customers' choices, decreasing these orders by 23 percent.[5]

In recent years, fast food chains have tried to address environmentalists' concerns by altering some of their business practices. Burger King renovated many of its locations with new technology and building materials to reduce electricity consumption by up to 90 percent.[6] Similarly, McDonald's has installed lights, kitchen equipment, and hand dryers that use less energy.

Despite public relations announcements about their goals for reducing greenhouse gas emissions, chains have often fallen short of meeting them. For instance, McDonald's promised to reduce its emissions to zero by 2050. However, a *New York Times* report in 2023 found that its emissions in 2021 were 12 percent higher than they were in 2015.[7]

Activists in Belgium demonstrated in front of a McDonald's in 2023, highlighting the amount of material used in the company's packaging.

TOO MUCH PACKAGING

Environmentalists have also long found fault with fast food chains for their packaging. Used fast food bags, wrappers, and boxes make up an estimated 20 percent of all litter found on city streets and along highways.[8] Much of the plastic pollution in the world's oceans comes from discarded single-use food and beverage packaging.

Fast food chains have responded by changing their packaging. For instance, McDonald's announced in 2018 that it was working toward making all its packaging from renewable and recycled sources. Some chains, such as Starbucks, are also encouraging customers to recycle used packaging by setting up recycling bins in their locations. In 2021, Burger King began testing reusable containers for sandwiches, drinks, and coffee in select cities. Customers are charged a deposit for the containers. If they bring the containers back to a Burger King, where they will be cleaned and used again, their deposit is refunded.

FOOD SWAMPS

Critics of fast food often note the high number of fast food restaurants in low-income communities. This concentration was not an accident. When fast food restaurants were looking for new markets in the 1960s and 1970s, they began to establish outlets in poorer urban neighborhoods because

the federal government often provided funding for these
development efforts.

Today, low-income workers are sometimes stereotyped
as irresponsible for eating unhealthful fast food. But fast
food is actually more often consumed by people in the
middle and upper-middle classes, who have many more
food options available to them.
When low-income workers
patronize fast food restaurants,
it is often because they have
little choice.

Many low-income
Americans live in what are
called food swamps—areas
without a nearby supermarket but with several fast food
outlets. Supermarket chains, operating on a very low
profit margin, often do not want to open outlets in poorer
neighborhoods, fearing that they will lose money. People in
food swamps may have a few fast food restaurants within an
easy walk, but they may be miles from a supermarket where
they can buy fresh, healthful food. If they do not have a car
or if they are working multiple jobs, getting most meals at a
fast food restaurant seems a rational choice. However, that

In many places, fast food restaurants are much more readily available than markets that offer healthier options, with multiple fast food locations often clustered together.

choice can come with a great cost. Studies show that people living in food swamps are more likely to suffer from strokes and other health problems than people with ready access to supermarkets.

Some cities and countries are working to eliminate food swamps. They provide loans and assistance to food

businesses that want to open in underserved low-income areas. Local governments also organize programs to encourage corner stores to stock fresh produce and establish farmers markets that cater to people receiving food assistance from the federal government. Despite these innovations, food swamps persist.

CHAPTER SEVEN

HARD AT WORK

At 6:30 a.m. on November 29, 2012, workers at a McDonald's restaurant on Madison Avenue in New York City took to the streets. They shouted, "Hey, hey, what do you say? We demand fair pay."[1] Soon after, hundreds of employees from dozens of the city's other fast food restaurants walked off the job and joined the protest. The action was the culmination of months of planning by community groups and civil rights organizations. At the time, it was the largest protest by fast food workers ever staged in the United States.

One protester summed up the grievances to a reporter for the *New York Times*. He had been working at McDonald's for three years, and he was earning only $8 an hour, far below what could be considered a living wage in an expensive city like New York. The protester told the reporter, "It's time for a change."[2]

The 2010s saw multiple large-scale protests against McDonald's and other fast food chains. Many of these efforts were about raising the wages of fast food workers.

Many fast food workers earn so little money that they must rely on federal government programs to survive. For instance, they may qualify for Medicaid, which provides health care for people in poverty, and for SNAP, which helps people afford food. In a 2013 study, labor and economics researchers found that 52 percent of fast food employees such as cooks received benefits from at least one public assistance program, while only 25 percent of the total workforce did. From 2007 to 2011, the total public assistance to these workers and their families averaged nearly $7 billion a year.[4]

A rallying cry by the protesters also explained their situation: "How can we survive on seven twenty-five?" In 2012, the federal minimum wage was $7.25, and many fast food workers made little more. The protesters demanded a minimum wage of more than double that amount.[3] Their movement became known as the Fight for $15.

Many similar walkouts and protests followed in the United States. They not only drew attention to the plight of fast food workers but also sometimes yielded concrete results. By the beginning of 2024, seven states—Washington, Connecticut, Massachusetts, California, New York, New Jersey, and Maryland—and the District of Columbia had minimum wages of at least $15 an hour. Six others had resolved to increase their minimum wages to $15 an hour over time. But even with these gains, many American fast food workers continue to receive so little pay that they live in poverty despite working full-time jobs.

A HISTORY OF LOW WAGES

Throughout the history of the fast food industry, low wages have been central to its business model. The pioneers of fast food knew they had to keep employee pay down if they were to make a profit on their low-priced products. They purposely created operations where they could hire young, unskilled workers, usually on a temporary basis.

Initially, fast food employees were largely teenagers working at their first jobs. Instead of trying to earn a living, they were usually working for pocket money, so the low pay did not seem unfair to the public. Fast food chains further defended the low wages by saying that they were providing young people with a valuable, character-building experience by teaching them how to hold a job.

By the 1980s, there were fewer teenagers willing to work in fast food than there were positions available. Chains then began to hire another class of workers that could afford to work for low wages—retired workers living off Social Security or pensions. Fast food jobs were seen as a way of supplementing their fixed income. The industry also

The demographics of fast food workers have shifted over the years, with more seniors taking these jobs.

suggested that fast food jobs benefited senior Americans by giving them contact with customers and fellow employees, thus alleviating any social isolation.

During the early 2000s, many fast food workers have been recent immigrants and people from other marginalized populations. They often take these low-paying jobs simply because no other work is available to them. Most of these workers are no longer teens. By 2023, the average fast food employee was 26 years old. About 64 percent of fast food workers were women, and many workers were Black, Hispanic, or Asian. The average hourly wage they earned was $13.53.[5] More than 25 percent of fast food employees were responsible for financially supporting a child on this income.[6]

SCHEDULING HEADACHES

Low pay is only one of many difficulties fast food workers face. Most also receive none of the benefits that often come with full-time work, including medical insurance, paid sick leave, paid vacation, and childcare benefits. Fast food employees also report wage theft—that is, being made to perform unpaid work. It is not uncommon for restaurant managers to require employees to work before or after their official shifts, to deny them overtime pay as required by law, or to make them work during legally mandated breaks.

In recent years, digital monitoring has made fast food work more stressful. If employees are not performing their tasks fast enough, monitoring systems automatically alert their managers. Workers' schedules are now also controlled by computers and are designed to provide the smallest number of employees possible to serve the customers expected at every hour. The system ensures that restaurants are always slightly understaffed, requiring employees to work at a frenzied pace during peak times.

> **In 2021, fast food chains employed about 3.3 million people in the United States.[7]**

Workers' schedules also vary from week to week. They usually receive schedules only a few days in advance, making it difficult to plan events in their personal lives. Even with schedules in place, workers cannot be sure of the hours they will be asked to work.

Managers often expect employees to be on call to work if the restaurant becomes unexpectedly busy, and they frequently send workers home early if business is slow. Employees sometimes find themselves scheduled to "clopen"—to close the restaurant late at night and then open it early the following morning, leaving only a few hours for sleep.

In early 2024, the job review website Glassdoor issued its annual "Best Places to Work" ranking. Out of 100 American companies listed, only one fast food chain made the cut. California's In-N-Out Burger came in at number six, ranking higher than tech giants Google and Apple. In-N-Out is unusual in the fast food industry for offering workers a host of benefits, including medical and dental insurance, life insurance, profit sharing, paid vacation and sick days, and free meals.

HAZARDOUS WORKPLACES

At many fast food restaurants, workers must deal with dangerous working conditions. Among their complaints are overflowing sewage, smoke inhalation, and extreme heat.

Pressure to work hard and fast leads to injuries, particularly sprained ankles and bruises caused by falling on wet or greasy floors. Burns from contact with frying equipment are also extremely common. A 2015 survey of fast food workers conducted by the National Council for Occupational Safety and Health found that in one year 79 percent of fast food workers had suffered burns, sometimes more than once.[8]

Workers are also in danger of becoming victims of crime. With restaurants open late at night, robberies are common, particularly at drive-throughs, where thieves can easily make a fast getaway. Many female fast food workers also experience sexual harassment and assault from both fellow employees and customers.

Many fast food chains use deep fryers. Mistakes or accidents can cause severe burns from the hot oil.

A study published in 2016 showed that 40 percent of women in nonmanagerial fast food jobs had been the victim of unwanted sexual attention in the workplace.[9] Female workers may be discouraged from reporting sexual harassment, fearing that their superiors will punish them by cutting their hours and assigning them undesirable jobs.

TAKING ACTION

Fast food chains have long fought efforts to address these issues. For instance, they have lobbied against hikes in the minimum wage, new regulations to ensure worker safety, and requirements for paid sick leave. They have also quashed workers' attempts to form unions that could negotiate higher pay and better working conditions. While about 10 percent of American workers are unionized, less than 1 percent of fast food workers are.[10]

Unionizing fast food restaurants is especially difficult because many workers are not invested in the work as a career. High job turnover and the large

One of fast food workers' greatest challenges is dealing with abusive customers. A 2021 report analyzed 911 call logs in California's nine largest cities. It found that fast food restaurants were the site of 77,000 violent and threatening incidents between 2017 and 2020.[11] Interviews detailed workers' experiences of being punched, choked, and pelted with food and drinks. Most outlets do not have a security guard, and few workers are trained to deal with customer violence. Restaurants also rarely pay for medical treatment because of injuries or offer mental health assistance to deal with psychological trauma.

number of part-time workers create challenges for union organizers. Nevertheless, since 2021, the union Workers United has organized about 400 Starbucks outlets.[12]

Advocates for fast food workers have had more success with getting governments to pass laws to improve their pay. In 2023, California passed Assembly Bill 1228, the result of lengthy negotiations between Governor Gavin Newsom, the Service Employees International Union (SEIU), and fast food companies operating in the state. The law, which set a new minimum wage of $20 an hour specifically for fast food workers, went into

California assemblymember Chris Holden was among the officials pushing for Assembly Bill 1228, which set a higher minimum wage for fast food workers.

effect on April 1, 2024. Critics of the change suggested it could lead to job losses and higher prices for consumers.

CHAPTER EIGHT

THE FUTURE OF FAST FOOD

Taco Bell's Defy restaurant opened in June 2022 in Brooklyn Park, Minnesota. Decorated in neon purple, it looked a little like a futuristic checkpoint on a toll highway. On top of the two-story structure was a large kitchen. On the lower story were four drive-through lanes—one for delivery drivers and three for customers who had placed orders using the chain's app. When each car reached the delivery window, a circular tray with the customer's order descended from the kitchen in a small tube-shaped elevator. By design, Defy delivered fast food orders in minutes without the customer ever seeing an employee.

Only a few years before, fast food drive-throughs were facing a popular backlash. Activists spoke out against them, citing them as threats to pedestrian safety and contributors to greenhouse

At Taco Bell's highly automated Defy restaurant, the company tested high-tech concepts it could roll out more widely in the future.

gas emissions and street noise. In fact, in 2019, the city of Minneapolis, located just a few miles from the Defy restaurant, banned the construction of new drive-throughs. The quick turnaround from banning drive-throughs to constructing turbocharged versions of them stemmed from a crisis in the fast food industry sparked by the start of the COVID-19 pandemic.

EMBRACING THE DRIVE-THROUGH

To slow the spread of COVID-19, many restaurants were forced to close their dining areas beginning in March 2020. At the same time, fast food outlets were facing staffing problems as their employees began quitting, not willing to risk their health for the low wages they were being paid. During the early days of the pandemic, many restaurants faced financial ruin, but most fast food outlets were able to survive and thrive because of their drive-throughs, which they could keep in operation even with reduced staff. Customers, even dine-in regulars, came to fully embrace drive-through pickup.

> **By the end of 2021, diners ate inside the restaurant on only 14 percent of fast food visits.[1]**

Even after the COVID-19 vaccine decreased the chance of serious illness, people continued to frequent drive-throughs. By 2022, 85 percent of all fast food orders were takeout, and 75 percent were drive-through pickups.[2] To keep up with demand, chains started focusing mostly on drive-throughs, which allowed them to reduce the size of their dining rooms and save on real estate costs. A new McDonald's that opened in Fort Worth, Texas, in late 2022 reflected this trend. It was the first outlet the chain had opened in many years without a dining room.

Fast casual restaurants had always tried to distinguish themselves from fast food outlets by offering a better dine-in experience. But they still began to copy fast food's drive-through model. For instance, beginning in 2021, Chipotle heavily promoted the "Chipotlane" built in nearly all its new restaurants.

Even as the initial COVID-19 threat subsided, fast food drive-throughs remained popular for several reasons. Some customers who had frequented drive-throughs during the pandemic got used to buying fast food that way and continued to do so out of habit. The pandemic may have made some customers less comfortable dealing with strangers and more likely to embrace drive-through options.

Many fast food employees received masks and gloves early in the COVID-19 pandemic, but the disease outbreak also led to changes in the fast food business that lasted for years afterward.

Another reason was more practical. During the pandemic, fast food restaurants were forced to make upgrades to improve their drive-through systems. For instance, some outlets reorganized kitchens to put together drive-through orders more quickly and rethought their parking lots to improve traffic management.

Another pandemic-inspired trend that continued was the rise in fast food delivery orders. During the pandemic, many customers ordered fast food through third-party delivery services such as DoorDash and Uber Eats, forcing chains to develop new packaging and containers to keep food from becoming cold or soggy in transit. Delivery was generally more expensive, sometimes as much as double the price of drive-through pickup, but some customers were willing to pay more for the convenience.

DIGITAL ORDERING

The disruption caused by the pandemic compelled the fast food industry to reduce staffing. One effect of this has been the skyrocketing use of digital ordering. By October 2023, McDonald's announced that 40 percent of its orders were taken digitally through apps and websites on computers and smartphones.[3]

Chains have also made it easier to place digital orders in person. To facilitate drive-through ordering, Starbucks and Chick-fil-A have sent employees with computer tablets to take orders from customers waiting in their cars. Chick-fil-A has also embraced at-table digital ordering, where diners place their orders on table-side tablets.

Many chains also allow customers to place digital orders at kiosks rather than by speaking to a worker at the counter. Kiosks offer several advantages to customers. They can display the menu in different languages and inform the customers how to redeem rewards in chains' loyalty programs. Customers also like to use kiosks because they can scroll through the menu offerings at their leisure without feeling rushed. Chains benefit because the longer customers peruse the menu, the more items they are likely to order.

For many decades, the intercom ordering systems at conventional drive-throughs barely changed, even though both customers and employees complained that they often malfunctioned. Chains are now beginning to improve these systems by using artificial intelligence (AI) to recognize spoken customer orders or even respond with computer-generated voices. AI order-taking systems may one day be used for movie and television promotional tie-ins by speaking in the voice of a celebrity or character.

DRONE DELIVERY

In November 2023 at a central Florida location, Chick-fil-A began offering customers using its app the option to have their food delivered by drone. At the restaurant, drone orders are packed into a cardboard box and affixed to the flying device. The drone then flies to the destination and lowers the order on a cable, where it can be retrieved by the customer.

Current drive-through AI systems, however, have some common glitches. Windy conditions or overhearing orders from nearby drive-through lanes can cause these systems to get orders wrong. Significant work will be needed to make AI drive-through ordering a mainstream practice.

ROBOT HELPERS

In recent years, many chains have experimented with using robots to serve, deliver, and make their products. For instance, in 2023, Wendy's announced that it was building underground pipes at some outlets. Robots could use these pipes to deliver drive-through orders to cars parked in spaces designated as "instant pickup portals."[4]

But the chain perhaps most interested in robot technology is Chick-fil-A, which has used robots to deliver food to tables in its restaurants, freeing up time for dining room employees to concentrate on refilling soft drinks and cleaning tables. Starting in 2022, Chick-fil-A tested robotic vehicles for delivering orders outside its restaurants. The vehicles' depth-perception cameras allowed them to navigate streets and sidewalks at up to 15 miles per hour (24 kmh). During the testing phase, however, the robots were accompanied by "safety chasers" who were there to make

Robots could help improve safety for fast food employees, taking on dangerous tasks such as operating fryers.

sure the robots operated properly and to answer questions from curious passersby.[5]

Robots are also taking over routine kitchen duties. The fast casual restaurant Chipotle is experimenting with the use of the Autocado to make its guacamole. This robot takes over the tedious tasks of cutting, coring, and peeling avocados. A human employee then steps in and hand-mashes the fruits to finish the guacamole.

Even more ambitious is the Infinite Kitchen, which the Sweetgreen salad chain began using at select outlets in 2023. Its robot assembly line has tubes that dispense

50 ingredients to make 500 salads an hour, about 50 percent

more than a team of human workers can produce.[6] A small staff of employees, however, remains on hand to prep ingredients, help customers with kiosk orders, and put the finishing touches on the salads served.

One of the companies most active in building robots for the fast food industry is Miso Robotics. It invested $50 million to develop Flippy the Robot, which was originally designed to cook hamburgers.[7] Flippy has since been adapted to run the fryer station, traditionally the area where most workplace accidents occur, at more than a dozen White Castle restaurants. Other robots created by Miso Robotics include Chippy, which makes tortilla chips at Chipotle, and Sippy, which pours and seals beverages at Jack in the Box.

CELLULAR AGRICULTURE

In the future, a fast food burger may not always start with a cow. It might be grown from animal stem cells in a process called cellular agriculture. In 2013 at Maastricht University in the Netherlands, a team of researchers created the first burger patty using this new technology. Although many companies are investing heavily in cellular agriculture, lab-grown beef and chicken have been too expensive to sell commercially. But one day, they could become a staple of fast food menus.

AT A CROSSROADS

In California in late December 2023, Miso Robotics collaborated on opening a new restaurant called CaliExpress by Flippy. Orders are taken at kiosks and prepared by a pair of Flippys—one that grills burgers and one that cooks french fries. It is thought to be the first fully automated restaurant in the world.

While increased automation in the fast food industry seems inevitable, questions remain about how well these systems will work. Will people and robots be able to work together? Will human employees resent corporations for shifting jobs to robots? Will customers still enjoy a fast food experience with little or no human interaction?

What is clear is that the fast food industry will continue finding ways to adapt to an evolving world. For decades,

ROBOT-MADE PIZZA

In 2015, Zume was ready to shake up the pizza delivery industry. The California company raised $445 million from investors.[8] People were impressed by its plan to assemble an army of food trucks in which robots would cook pizzas to order while the trucks traveled to the customers' homes. The venture, however, did not work as planned. One central problem was that cheese kept sliding off the pizzas when the trucks went over bumpy roads. In 2023, Zume admitted defeat and closed up shop.

it has weathered a host of challenges. The industry has addressed changing tastes and health concerns. It has adjusted its menus and restaurants to match the culinary and social norms of other cultures. It has made changes in response to critics of its environmental and employment policies. It has even survived a global pandemic. Since its invention, the fast food industry has always been able to identify what its consumers want and keep them coming back for more.

WHAT IS FAST FOOD?

- Fast food is food that is prepared quickly and efficiently and sold at an inexpensive price.

- Fast food was once considered uniquely American, but now it is a global phenomenon. There are an estimated one million fast food outlets around the world.

- Fast food chains frequently add new food items to their menus to appeal to customers' desire for novelty and to remain competitive in the industry.

FAST FOOD HISTORY

- White Castle, the first American fast food chain, was established in Kansas in 1921.

- Drawing on the efficiencies engineered by restaurateurs Dick and Mac McDonald, Ray Kroc created the model for modern fast food chains through his development of McDonald's starting in the 1950s.

- Following World War II, an economic boom allowed more American families to buy cars and move to the suburbs. In the 1950s and 1960s, fast food chains were designed to cater particularly to suburban families and travelers on the country's new highway system.

- Since the 1960s, much of fast food marketing has been designed to appeal directly to children. Black and Hispanic young people are particularly targeted.

ISSUES AND CONTROVERSIES

- Nutritional experts decry the large amounts of fat, salt, and sugar in fast food. Fast food has been attacked for feeding customers "empty calories."

- Activists criticize the fast food industry for contributing to poor living conditions for livestock, for playing a role in climate change, and for creating trash through excess packaging.

- Food swamps—areas where there are several fast food outlets but no readily accessible supermarkets—make it challenging for residents of some low-income communities to eat a healthful diet.

- Fast food employees have traditionally been among the lowest-paid sectors of workers. Increasingly, they have been using protests to demand higher wages and aiming to unionize to improve their working conditions.

FAST FOOD TODAY

- The global COVID-19 pandemic of the early 2020s created a crisis in the restaurant industry. Fast food chains successfully weathered the storm by emphasizing drive-through orders, an industry trend that continued after the pandemic faded.

- In recent years, the fast food industry has begun exploring robotics, AI, and other new technologies to reduce the cost of staffing and make operations more efficient.

QUOTE

"During a relatively brief period of time, the fast food industry has helped to transform not only the American diet, but also our landscape, economy, workforce, and popular culture. Fast food and its consequences have become inescapable."

—*Eric Schlosser,* Fast Food Nation

GLOSSARY

artificial intelligence (AI)
Computer systems that can learn, write, analyze, and perform other tasks associated with human intelligence.

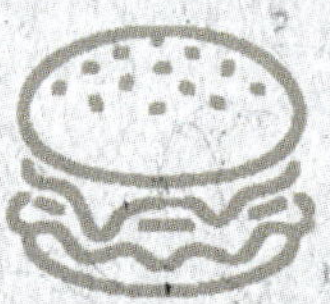

cuisine
The cooking methods and food traditions of a particular group of people.

diabetes
A health condition caused by a lack of the hormone insulin, leading to high levels of sugar in the blood and urine.

drone
A small remote-controlled flying machine.

entrée
The main course or main dish in a meal.

franchise
A business that uses a concept and name created by a parent company, usually in exchange for an initial fee and a percentage of the ongoing sales.

franchisee
A person or company that franchises a business concept from a parent company.

integrity
Adhering to a set of moral principles.

living wage
A wage that provides enough income to purchase the necessities of life, such as housing and food.

marginalize
To treat a person or group as though they are unimportant.

marketing
Promoting a product or service to encourage customers to purchase it.

methodology
A set of rules used when engaging in a certain activity.

minimum wage
The lowest hourly wage a worker can receive, as mandated by a government.

pandemic
The outbreak of disease over a large area.

preservative
A substance added to food to keep it from spoiling.

renewable
Capable of being replaced after use.

trans fat
A type of fatty acid found in margarine and some cooking oils that, when consumed, can cause plaque to build up in a person's arteries.

union
A workers' organization charged with negotiating pay rates with companies and otherwise looking out for the workers' interests.

SELECTED BIBLIOGRAPHY

Chandler, Adam. *Drive-Thru Dreams: A Journey through the Heart of America's Fast-Food Kingdom*. Flatiron, 2019.

Park, Alex. "What Fast Food Tells Us about the World." *Current Affairs*, 25 Jan. 2021, currentaffairs.org. Accessed 27 Jan. 2024.

Schlosser, Eric. *Fast Food Nation: The Dark Side of the All-American Meal*. Mariner, 2001.

FURTHER READINGS

Allman, Toney. *Living a Healthy Lifestyle*. ReferencePoint, 2020.

Burling, Alexis. *Food Delivery*. Abdo, 2025.

Waldendorf, Kurt. *Food Marketing*. Abdo, 2025.

ONLINE RESOURCES

To learn more about fast food, please visit **abdobooklinks.com** or scan this QR code. These links are routinely monitored and updated to provide the most current information available.

CHAPTER 1. FAST, CHEAP, AND TASTY

1. Steven Mark Adelson. "McDonald's and the New Franchising Paradigm." *Financial History*, Summer 2012, moaf.org. Accessed 14 Feb. 2024.

2. Adelson, "McDonald's and the New Franchising Paradigm."

3. Adelson, "McDonald's and the New Franchising Paradigm."

4. Adam Chandler. *Drive-Thru Dreams*. Kindle ed., Flatiron, 2019.

5. Adelson, "McDonald's and the New Franchising Paradigm."

6. Andrew F. Smith. *Fast Food: The Good, the Bad and the Hungry*. Kindle ed., Reaktion, 2016.

7. "US Inflation Calculator." *US Inflation Calculator*, 2024, usinflationcalculator.com. Accessed 20 June 2024.

8. Adelson, "McDonald's and the New Franchising Paradigm."

9. Ray Kroc with Robert Anderson. *Grinding It Out: The Making of McDonald's*. Macmillan, 1987. 6.

10. Kroc, *Grinding It Out*, 7.

11. Kroc, *Grinding It Out*, 7.

12. Kroc, *Grinding It Out*, 9.

13. Thomas Riggs, ed. *St. James Encyclopedia of Popular Culture*. Cengage Learning, 2013. 280.

14. Adelson, "McDonald's and the New Franchising Paradigm."

15. "Restaurants by Country." *McDonald's*, 2022, corporate.mcdonalds.com. Accessed 20 June 2024.

16. Smith, *Fast Food*.

17. "Fast Food Consumption among Adults in the United States." *Centers for Disease Control and Prevention*, 30 Oct. 2018, cdc.gov. Accessed 20 June 2024.

CHAPTER 2. ON THE GO

1. Elisabetta Povoledo. "Snail, Fish and Sheep Soup, Anyone? Savory New Finds at Pompeii." *New York Times*, 28 Dec. 2020, nytimes.com. Accessed 6 Mar. 2024.

2. Adam Chandler. *Drive-Thru Dreams*. Kindle ed., Flatiron, 2019.

3. Fred Grandinetti. "90 Years with J. Wellington Wimpy." *Boomer*, 27 July 2021, boomermagazine.com. Accessed 6 Mar. 2024.

4. Andrew F. Smith. *Fast Food: The Good, the Bad and the Hungry*. Kindle ed., Reaktion, 2016.

5. Chandler, *Drive-Thru Dreams*.

6. Laura Reiley and Lee Powell. "The Robots Are Here. And They Are Making You Fries." *Washington Post*, 20 Sept. 2022, washingtonpost.com. Accessed 20 June 2024.

7. Edith Evans Asbury. "Col. Harland Sanders, Founder of Kentucky Fried Chicken, Dies." *New York Times*, 17 Dec. 1980, timesmachine.nytimes.com. Accessed 13 Mar. 2024.

8. J. Y. Smith. "Col. Sanders, the Fried-Chicken Gentleman, Dies." *Washington Post*, 17 Dec. 1980, washingtonpost.com. Accessed 20 June 2024.

9. "Fatburger." *Fat Brands*, n.d., fatbrands.com. Accessed 20 June 2024.

CHAPTER 3. CONQUERING THE WORLD

1. Adam Chandler. *Drive-Thru Dreams*. Kindle ed., Flatiron, 2019.

2. Andrew F. Smith. *Fast Food: The Good, the Bad and the Hungry*. Kindle ed., Reaktion, 2016.

3. Julie Creswell. "McDonald's, Coca-Cola and Starbucks Temporarily Stop Sales in Russia." *New York Times*, 8 Mar. 2022, nytimes.com. Accessed 20 June 2024.

4. "The History of Slow Food." *Slow Food USA*, n.d., slowfoodusa.org. Accessed 24 Feb. 2024.

5. "Fast Food Market Share." *T4*, 23 Dec. 2022, t4.ai. Accessed 24 Feb. 2024.

6. Chandler, *Drive-Thru Dreams*.

7. Alex Park. "What Fast Food Tells Us about the World." *Current Affairs*, 25 Jan. 2021, currentaffairs.org. Accessed 27 Jan. 2024.

CHAPTER 4. KEEPING CUSTOMERS HAPPY

1. K. Annabelle Smith. "The Fishy History of the McDonald's Filet-O-Fish Sandwich." *Smithsonian Magazine*, 1 Mar. 2013, smithsonianmag.com. Accessed 20 June 2024.

2. Smith, "History of Filet-O-Fish."

3. Smith, "History of Filet-O-Fish."

4. Smith, "History of Filet-O-Fish."

5. Thomas Riggs, ed. *St. James Encyclopedia of Popular Culture*. Cengage Learning, 2013. 281.

6. Adam Chandler. *Drive-Thru Dreams*. Kindle ed., Flatiron, 2019.

7. "Dave Thomas, Founder of Wendy's, Dies at 69." *New York Times*, 8 Jan. 2002, nytimes.com. Accessed 20 June 2024.

8. Riggs, *St. James Encyclopedia of Popular Culture*, 282.

9. Kristin Messina. "Rudd Center: New Study Finds Fast-Food Companies Spending More on Advertising, Disproportionately Targeting Black and Latino Youth." *UConn Today*, 17 June 2021, today.uconn.edu. Accessed 20 June 2024.

10. Andrew F. Smith. *Fast Food: The Good, the Bad and the Hungry*. Kindle ed., Reaktion, 2016.

11. Smith, *Fast Food*.

CHAPTER 5. NUTRITION WOES

1. "The Dark Side of 'Super Size.'" *NBC News*, 18 May 2004, nbcnews.com. Accessed 7 Mar. 2024.

2. Jacqueline Stenson. "Calorie Counts on Menus: Have They Helped?" *NBC News*, 11 June 2022, nbcnews.com. Accessed 8 Mar. 2024.

3. Adam Chandler. *Drive-Thru Dreams*. Kindle ed., Flatiron, 2019.

4. Andrew F. Smith. *Fast Food: The Good, the Bad and the Hungry*. Kindle ed., Reaktion, 2016.

5. Smith, *Fast Food*.

6. Sommer Mathis. "Everything You Need to Know about the New York Soda Ban." *Bloomberg*, 13 Sept. 2012, bloomberg.com. Accessed 8 Mar. 2024.

7. Sam Oches. "The Bloomberg Precedent." *QSR*, 14 Jan. 2013, qsrmagazine.com. Accessed 8 Mar. 2024.

8. "Nutrition Calculator." *McDonald's*, n.d., mcdonalds.com. Accessed 7 Mar. 2024.

9. "Interactive Nutrition Menu." *Kentucky Fried Chicken*, n.d., kfc.com. Accessed 7 Mar. 2024.

10. "Nutritional Information." *Burger King*, n.d., bk.com. Accessed 7 Mar. 2024.

11. "Full Nutrition Info." *Taco Bell*, n.d., tacobell.com. Accessed 7 Mar. 2024.

12. David Stout. "Judge Rejects Obese Teenagers' Suit against McDonald's." *New York Times*, 22 Jan. 2003, nytimes.com. Accessed 8 Mar. 2024.

13. Smith, *Fast Food*.

14. Chandler, *Drive-Thru Dreams*.

15. Richard Gibson. "McDonald's Skinny Burger Is a Hard Sell." *Wall Street Journal*, 21 Apr. 1993, archive.seattletimes.com. Accessed 8 Mar. 2024.

16. Danielle E. Schoffman et al. "The Fast-Casual Conundrum: Fast-Casual Restaurant Entrées Are Higher in Calories than Fast Food." *Journal of the Academy of Nutrition and Dietetics*, vol. 116, no. 10, 1606–1612.

17. Smith, *Fast Food*.

CHAPTER 6. HIDDEN HARMS

1. Eric Schlosser. *Fast Food Nation: The Dark Side of the All-American Meal*. Mariner, 2012. 3.

2. Andrew F. Smith. *Fast Food: The Good, the Bad and the Hungry*. Kindle ed., Reaktion, 2016.

3. Kenny Torrella. "Big Food Is Ready to Sell You More Plant-Based Meat." *Vox*, 21 Jan. 2020, vox.com. Accessed 9 Mar. 2024.

4. Torrella, "Plant-Based Meat."

5. Erin Prater. "Fast Food Joints Can Help Battle Climate Change, New Study Finds." *FortuneWell*, 7 Jan. 2023, fortune.com. Accessed 27 Jan. 2024.

6. Smith, *Fast Food*.

7. Julie Creswell. "For Many Big Food Companies, Emissions Head in the Wrong Direction." *New York Times*, 24 Sept. 2023, nytimes.com. Accessed 9 Mar. 2024.

8. Smith, *Fast Food*.

9. Max Holleran. "How Fast Food Chains Supersized Inequality." *New Republic*, 2 Aug. 2017, newrepublic.com. Accessed 9 Mar. 2024.

CHAPTER 7. HARD AT WORK

1. Steven Greenhouse. "With Day of Protests, Fast-Food Workers Seek More Pay." *New York Times*, 29 Nov. 2012, nytimes.com. Accessed 11 Mar. 2024.

2. Steven Greenhouse. "In Drive to Unionize, Fast-Food Workers Walk Off the Job." *New York Times*, 28 Nov. 2012, nytimes.com. Accessed 11 Mar. 2024.

3. Greenhouse, "Fast-Food Workers Walk Off the Job."

4. Sylvia Allegretto et al. "Fast Food, Poverty Wages." *UC Berkeley Labor Center*, 15 Oct. 2013, laborcenter.berkeley.edu. Accessed 12 Mar. 2024.

5. Nancy Luna. "Meet the Typical Fast-Food Worker." *Business Insider*, 22 Dec. 2023, businessinsider.com. Accessed 11 Mar. 2024.

6. Emily Guendelsberger. "I Was a Fast-Food Worker. Let Me Tell You about Burnout." *Vox*, 15 July 2019, vox.com. Accessed 20 Jan. 2024.

7. Luna, "Meet the Typical Fast-Food Worker."

8. Guendelsberger, "I Was a Fast-Food Worker."

9. Bryce Covert. "McDonald's Has a Real Sexual Harassment Problem." *Nation*, 28 July 2020, thenation.com. Accessed 11 Mar. 2024.

10. Bob Woods. "How McDonald's, Chipotle, Starbucks Are Preparing for the Fast-Food Worker Battles to Come in 2024." *CNBC*, 29 Dec. 2023, cnbc.com. Accessed 11 Mar. 2024.

11. Jessica Fu. "Fast Food Workers Are Using 911 Call Logs to Draw Attention to a Hidden 'Crisis of Violence.'" *Counter*, 14 Dec. 2021, thecounter.org. Accessed 12 Mar. 2024.

12. Waylon Cunningham and Daniel Wiessner. "Starbucks Union Seeks National Template for US Bargaining." *Reuters*, 1 Mar. 2024, reuters.com. Accessed 12 Mar. 2024.

CHAPTER 8. THE FUTURE OF FAST FOOD

1. Whizy Kim. "You May Never Eat inside a Fast-Food Restaurant Again." *Vox*, 5 May 2023, vox.com. Accessed 20 Jan. 2024.

2. Kim, "You May Never Eat inside a Fast-Food Restaurant Again."

3. Kim Severson. "Hungry (But Not for Human Contact), Americans Head for the Drive-Through." *New York Times*, 7 Nov. 2023, nytimes.com. Accessed 13 Mar. 2024.

4. Harry Guinness. "Wendy's Wants Underground Robots to Deliver Food to Your Car." *Popular Science*, 18 May 2023, popsci.com. Accessed 13 Mar. 2024.

5. "The Future of Delivery Is Here." *Chick-fil-A*, 31 May 2022, chick-fil-a.com. Accessed 13 Mar. 2024.

6. Nancy Luna. "Robots Are Taking Over Fast-Food Kitchens." *Business Insider*, 24 Dec. 2023, businessinsider.com. Accessed 13 Mar. 2024.

7. Laura Reiley and Lee Powell. "The Robots Are Here. And They Are Making You Fries." *Washington Post*, 20 Sept. 2022, washingtonpost.com. Accessed 20 June 2024.

8. Stephen Council. "Bay Area-Founded Pizza Startup Zume Reportedly Shuts Down after Raising $445 Million." *San Francisco Gate*, 5 June 2023, sfgate.com. Accessed 14 Mar. 2024.

LIZ SONNEBORN

A graduate of Swarthmore College, Liz Sonneborn has written more than 100 books for young readers and adults on a wide variety of subjects. Her specialties include American history, world history, biography, women's studies, and African American studies. Sonneborn is a longtime resident of Brooklyn, New York.